FRENCH PAINTING AND SCULPTURE
OF THE XVIII CENTURY

FRENCH
PAINTING
AND
SCULPTURE
OF THE
XVIII CENTURY

AN EXHIBITION, *November 6, 1935*
through January 5, 1936

LIST OF LENDERS

ANONYMOUS

JULES S. BACHE

MME JACQUES BALSAN

EDWARD J. BERWIND

ALBERT BLUM

GEORGE BLUMENTHAL

CALIFORNIA PALACE OF THE LEGION OF HONOR

COMTE ALLARD DU CHOLLET

COMÉDIE FRANÇAISE

D. DAVID-WEILL

MRS. HENRY P. DAVISON

HENRI ÉTIENNE DESTREM

PRINCESSE DE FAUCIGNY-LUCINGE

MRS. FRANK GRAY GRISWOLD

ESTATE OF MRS. J. HORACE HARDING

EDWARD S. HARKNESS

MR. AND MRS. CHARLES V. HICKOX

MRS. JULIAN HUMPHREYS

MRS. MARJORIE POST HUTTON

HENRY P. McILHENNY

ANDREW W. MELLON

MISS CAROLINE L. MORGAN

J. P. MORGAN

MUSÉE COGNACQ-JAY

MUSÉE DU LOUVRE

MUSÉE DE VERSAILLES

MUSEUM OF FINE ARTS, BOSTON

WILLIAM ROCKHILL NELSON GALLERY OF ART

MRS. ALEXANDER HAMILTON RICE

MRS. JOHN D. ROCKEFELLER, JR.

BARON HENRI DE ROTHSCHILD

BARON MAURICE DE ROTHSCHILD

DR. PRESTON POPE SATTERWHITE

JOHN M. SCHIFF

MRS. ROBERT W. SCHUETTE

JAMES SPEYER

EMIL J. STEHLI

MRS. HERBERT N. STRAUS

ESTATE OF JOHN R. THOMPSON

MRS. WILLIAM R. TIMKEN

WADSWORTH ATHENEUM

MRS. ELISHA WALKER

FORSYTH WICKES

JOSEPH E. WIDENER

PREFACE

AMERICANS have long been amateurs of the art of France. While those of the eighteenth century with few exceptions were too profoundly occupied with the foundation of a new country to concern themselves with art, once their country had gone through its formative period they turned to the old world for artistic interests. The echoes of our Revolutionary War were hardly stilled when Houdon gained patrons in America; and in the nineteenth century, first the decorative arts of the Empire, then French architecture, and finally, after our Civil War, French painting of each succeeding generation found in America enthusiastic admirers and collectors.

Meanwhile, in the last decade or two of the nineteenth century, there were many in America in whom a sympathetic chord was struck as they came to know the gay, urbane, and highly sophisticated art of the *ancien régime*. From what was at first popular merely as a style of decoration, there grew a collector's appreciation of the painting and sculpture contemporary with it, and, as time has gone on, those in America who have acquired works of this period have secured some of its finest examples.

The present exhibition is thus representative of a school which has had an important influence in this country. It is a striking fact that the Metropolitan Museum has been able to assemble from American collections works of the great majority of the significant painters and sculptors of eighteenth-century France. A few names were lacking, but fortunately the plans for the exhibition created an interest in France and what gaps there might have been were filled by the generosity of French institutions and collectors. This coöperation is all the more gratifying as showing the continued sympathy of the two nations in each other's artistic progress.

The names of those institutions and individuals to whom the Metropolitan Museum is indebted in the organization of the exhibition are given on pages v and vi. Mention should also be made of those French officials without whose assistance the exhibition would have lost much of its brilliancy: Georges Huisman, Directeur général des Beaux Arts; Henri Verne, Directeur des Musées Nationaux; Paul Jamot and Paul Vitry, Conservateurs au Musée du Louvre; Gaston Brière, Conservateur du Musée de Versailles; Émile Fabre, Administrateur de la Comédie Française; and Édouard Jonas, Conservateur du Musée Cognacq-Jay.

H. E. WINLOCK.

TABLE OF CONTENTS

FRENCH PAINTING AND SCULPTURE
OF THE XVIII CENTURY

FRENCH PAINTING *OF THE XVIII CENTURY*

THE transition from the heaviness of the Louis XIV style through the Regency to the wayward and vivacious style of Louis XV's reign was not so abrupt as might be supposed. In characterizing the arts of the epoch of Louis XIV, critics agree in stressing the importance of the Grand Monarque and his ministers as arbiters of taste. A style combining majesty with technical virtuosity was demanded, and there came into being an art which included something of the high spirit of Bernini's sculpture and something of the broad decorative quality of Bolognese painting, the whole rendered more official by the addition of a sort of ancient Roman nobility and banality. Versailles, with the unending grandeur of its park, its architecture, and its interior decorations, required a firm guiding principle.

In the field of painting a central fact was the czarlike position, the unassailable competence, the chilling academism of the king's painter Charles Le Brun. But the inventory will be incomplete if we minimize the importance of such independent geniuses as Nicolas Poussin and Claude Lorrain, whose abundant works were eagerly commissioned and bought by the cultivated laymen and clerics of the time. Even for the seventeenth-century painter success did not depend entirely on royal patronage. Like Poussin and Claude, the two splendid portraitists Hyacinthe Rigaud and Nicolas de Largillière were in great demand by private patrons who through their eager sympathies were already preparing the ground for new adventures in the arts.

Of these two portrait painters Largillière (1656-1746) was especially important as a revivifying agent. By the time his career was beginning Poussin and Claude were dead, and the imported Italian strain in painting had been running thin. Fresh impulses were needed and they came from Rubens's successors in the North. Van der Meulen had already brought a freer style and livelier color in his battle pictures and in his tapestry designs for the Gobelins looms.

3

Largillière augmented the Flemish influence. He had studied in Antwerp and later had worked under Lely in London. His portraits exhibited the somewhat operatic gestures demanded by the taste of the epoch, but there were a solid splendor in his figures and a richness of color and texture in his billowing fabrics that combined to make him a stimulating example (cf. figs. 1, 2). He worked industriously during the later decades of Louis XIV's reign, was at his best perhaps in painting the nobility and the prosperous bourgeoisie of the Regency, and continued active well into the reign of Louis XV.

Watteau (1684-1721), the greatest genius among painters of the eighteenth century, also brought ideas from the North. He was a native of Valenciennes, near the Flemish border, and his early style was based on Teniers. When first he came to Paris, in 1702, he worked in Claude Gillot's studio, where he delighted in subjects connected with the theater. Soon afterward as a privileged guest in the palace of a great Parisian collector he had an opportunity to study paintings and drawings by Rubens, Titian, and Veronese. His glorious painting Jupiter and Antiope (fig. 4), owned by the Louvre, shows Rubens's influence in its technical freedom, while the poetic beauty of the nude figure in its umbrageous setting points to Titian's famous painting of the same subject, which had been brought to Paris two generations earlier by the banker Jabach. But Titian's Venice would never have tolerated the appealing awkwardness of the sleeper's drooping arm, an intimacy in which we capture the very essence of the *dix-huitième siècle*.

Another of Watteau's masterpieces is Le Mezzetin (fig. 5), in which we observe a marvelous reconciliation of the real with the ideal. Beneath the fantastic player's costume we sense a lithe, strong body and an individualized personality. The setting, too, is a sufficiently believable eighteenth-century park, but the actualities of the picture have all been magically fused into a dreamlike, nostalgic melody.

In the Italian Serenade (fig. 3) Watteau again reverts to his fascinating theme of the Commedia dell' arte. His greatest contribution was, however, the related theme of the *fête galante*, seen to perfection in the Louvre's famous Embarkation for Cythera. Watteau's dainty lovers in their shimmering silks wear with slight modification the costumes of the time and disport themselves in a not unusual wood-land—as though a present-day artist were to paint the flirtations of a country club. But an air of tremulous romance pervades Watteau's scenes, and though their creator died prematurely in 1721, fashion-able France was not destined to abandon the delights of Cythera until the stern ideals of the Revolution loaded all such elegant dalliance into the tumbrels.

Watteau had two direct disciples. Pater (1695-1736), who closely followed his master's style, came down from Valenciennes to Paris and was taken into Watteau's studio. Some ten years after Watteau had been admitted into the Academy, Pater was accepted under the appellation "peintre de sujets modernes," perhaps in consideration of the new type of picture, the *fête galante*, or was it because of the con-temporaneity of the costuming? Although Pater died almost as young as Watteau he left us a great many paintings. They lack the enchant-ment and also the solider qualities of Watteau's work but are uni-formly harmonious. Some, like the Troops on the March and Troops at Rest (figs. 6, 7), teem with little figures and are ingeniously en-livened with alternating patches of light and shade. A few show a sketchier handling and a pale gray and rose scheme of color which Pater might have developed into an original style if he had lived longer.

Lancret (1690-1743), the other immediate disciple of Watteau, was a fellow pupil with him in Claude Gillot's atelier. He was a more original artist than Pater; one can observe in such paintings as The Duet (fig. 15) that he had a feeling for broader and simpler effects and kept his color clearer. The limbs of his figures do not always articu-late accurately and their faces are sometimes slightly out of drawing, but his types are his own and have an arresting way of seeming like real people. The Ham Lunch (fig. 12), a small study for or replica of the famous work he painted for Versailles, is a brilliant performance, full of sparkle and good humor. Another of his celebrated compositions is the large picture of Mlle Camargo Dancing (fig. 11), formerly in the collection of the German emperors.

To turn to Nattier (1685-1766) is to set back the clock, for his work has much of the pomp of the earlier reign. Watteau and his disciples had gone their own way and prospered without the court's active patronage, but Nattier, who was admitted to the Academy in the same year as Watteau, became a portraitist who found his clients among the great people of France. Like Van Dyck and Lely in England, he established a type of countenance to which his sitters were glad to be adjusted. His color was clear and pearly, though slightly fatigued. His ladies were often depicted as lovely goddesses and made to look as dignified as possible even when couched upon clouds. The portrait of the beautiful Mme Marsollier with her daughter (fig. 16) has a more intimate appeal than the deified ladies, and much of the amenity of Versailles today is due to similar handsome and kindly portraits of Marie Leczinska and her royal daughters (cf. fig. 19).

The occurrence of Chardin (1699-1779) in the field of French painting in the eighteenth century is comparable with the phenomenon of the simple-hearted Le Nain brothers in the seventeenth. He constitutes a refreshing variant which defies inclusion within the usual categories. The son of a cabinetmaker, Chardin was a kindly, unpretentious soul, a *bon papa* devoted to children and to the outward paraphernalia of tranquil domesticity. He developed a passion for painting familiar household things and did so in the stanch and simple way that accorded with his nature. Although he delighted in such domestic subjects as Grace before Meat (fig. 22) he had originally made his reputation with a picture of a dead sting ray, and to still-life painting he returned almost exclusively for the last quarter century of his career. His color is more peaceful and unified than that of the Dutch still-life painters, and the creamy texture of the pigment in some of his works may be compared with old maiolica or the pitted glazes of certain Sung porcelains.

As Nattier set the norm for portraiture so did Boucher (1703-1770) for decorative painting. As a young man he went to Italy, where he studied the works of Titian and Veronese and apparently learned much from Piazzetta's drawings and from the early decorations of Tiepolo, who was seven years his senior. By 1731 he was back in Paris and soon had established his style, opulent and suave in composition, light and transparent in color, an art flawless but not profound. It had for its subject matter the innocent amours of Arcady and the naked gods and the pink-toed nymphs and goddesses of Olympus (cf. figs. 28, 30). It was an art perfectly suited to the sophisticated taste of the time and to the bright, elegant interiors which it was intended to decorate. Boucher knew Mme de Pompadour even before 1745, in which year she was installed at Versailles, and executed many decorative commissions and portraits for her. For the royal tapestry factories he designed abundantly, and he became their director after Oudry's death in 1755.

It is not easy to do justice to the work of Greuze (1725-1805) because of the false sentiment and surreptitious sensuality which mar many of his pictures. During a visit to Italy at the age of thirty he painted Indolence (fig. 31), a skillful and objective picture of a young slattern amid the disorder of her natural surroundings. From about the same time dates The Broken Eggs (fig. 32), in which the symbolism of lost virtue is developed more playfully than in the celebrated Broken Pitcher. The Broken Eggs is by no means genuine drama, but at least the dice are not yet loaded in favor of virtue and old age as they are later in the homiletic Father's Curse and Son's Punishment. The painting is still slightly thin and brittle, but there is beauty in the figure of the sulky girl in her white dress. In the Girl Winding Yarn (fig. 33) appears the rich impasto of Greuze's maturer work, and in the Louvre's Dead Bird (fig. 34) is seen at her tenderest the innocently seductive child-woman upon whom Greuze doted. For his portraits, if for nothing else, Greuze must be admired even by his detractors, for here at least he is revealed with his sensitivity unmarred by sentimentality.

Any list of leading portrait painters of the century must also include the names of the two pastelists La Tour and Perronneau. La Tour was the more vivacious and original artist of the two, and it is to be regretted that the risk involved in transporting works in this medium has discouraged owners of his pastels from sending them to America. Perronneau (1715-1783), though his name is usually associated with pastels, was perhaps even more successful in his oils. Such a work as his portrait of the duchesse d'Ayen (fig. 38) reveals him as an excellent painter and an exquisitely sensitive psychologist.

One of the most dependable dynasties of French painters in the eighteenth century was the family Van Loo. Carle of the name, the outstanding member of the family, was director of the Academy and first painter to the king. He was much in demand not only for his official portraits but also for large projects involving religious and mythological subjects. A less prominent member of the family was Amédée Van Loo (1719-1795), who painted the original and delightful pair of pictures, The Soap Bubbles and The Magic Lantern (figs. 39, 40), said to portray his own children.

There were more generations than one of Drouais painters also. The most important of these, François Hubert Drouais (1727-1775), called Drouais le fils, painted portraits of many royal personages, including the delightful oval representation of Marie Antoinette (fig. 43) which shows her still in her teens. Drouais excelled in painting silks and laces and is famous especially for his charming pictures of children (cf. figs. 41, 42). The most famous of these is the Louvre's fresh and amusing portrait of the child comte d'Artois steadying his little sister on the back of a goat.

Each of Watteau's successors whom we have discussed, Pater, Lancret, Nattier, Chardin, Boucher, Greuze, Perronneau, Van Loo, and Drouais, added his special and precious contribution to the world's store of art. Each originated visual ideas which were in varying degrees new and capable of giving delight in their own time and subsequently. All were brilliant craftsmen. Connoisseurs there are without doubt who hold more than one of these to be geniuses, but no one has devised a means for detecting genius. The only test is our

own perceptions and emotions, and they seem to tell us that after
Watteau there was no French painter of genius until Chardin, and
after Chardin came Fragonard.

Fragonard (1732-1806) like most gifted people could dip up what
he needed from diverse sources. He studied with Chardin and later
worked in Boucher's atelier. In his own dashing technique he copied
the shadowy picture of the Holy Family with the Cradle by Rem-
brandt, which belonged to Crozat and later to Boucher. Almost from
the beginning Fragonard was more deeply absorbed in problems of
light and air than any French painter before, more effectively perhaps than any since. Enthusiastic patrons enabled him to extend to
nearly five years his student's term in Italy. As the guest of the abbé
de Saint-Non in the Villa d'Este at Tivoli he learned the beauty of
landscape under control. In Naples he took note of Solimena's distri-
bution of accents through a composition, in Venice he studied the
drawings and decorative paintings of Tiepolo. Where Boucher had
extracted profit simply from Tiepolo's joyous talent for tossing his
human elements into the clouds, Fragonard noted especially the
Venetian's dazzling genius for expressing his figures and his light in
terms of one another. In his finest decorations, such as the set in the
Frick Collection, in his Fête de Saint-Cloud, owned by the Bank of
France, and in his little figures of Love and Folly (figs. 47, 48) he
brings the captivating gaiety of dix-huitième painting for the second
time to a pitch of breathless perfection. The Reader (fig. 45) is so
delicate in color and so original that we do not at first notice the
mastery of form. The sportive Bathers (fig. 44) is such a tumultuous
composition of nude young bodies as France was not to know again
until Renoir. During his young manhood, when he moved in the un-
restrained society of dancers and prominent beauties, Frago tossed
off pictures of surprising piquancy, but the quality of the painting re-
mains always more engrossing than the subject matter, and even his
most sensual scenes are usually burned clean by the fire of genuine
passion. Later in life, settling down to marriage and responding to a
change in general taste, Fragonard devoted himself to such winsome

pictures of domestic life as The Love Letter (fig. 46) and The Happy Family (fig. 49). In these works he explored further than ever the beauty of contrasted light. But when, as occasionally happened, his stories overstressed virtue and childish innocence he could exceed the limits of good sense almost as sadly as could Greuze.

In 1760, when Fragonard was visiting the abbé de Saint-Non at Tivoli, his fellow guest was Hubert Robert (1733-1808). Robert had studied at the French Academy in Rome under Pannini, the great Italian painter of classical ruins. The pupil developed a lighter, fresher style than his teacher, a style perfectly adapted to the decoration of the chastely elegant interiors which had come into fashion under the reign of Louis XVI. The texture of Hubert Robert's ancient masonry is highly pleasurable, there is a cool tinkle from his fountains and a sweet airiness in his trees. In his informally arranged Terrace of the Château de Marly (fig. 53) the ladies are politely eager. His talent for composing pseudo-accidental landscapes made him not only a good picture maker but also the perfect designer for the *hameau* at Versailles where Marie Antoinette could play milkmaid.

A portrait painter of the time whose name we associate especially with Marie Antoinette is Mme Vigée Le Brun (1755-1842), whose professional career carried through the Revolution, the Empire, and beyond. As Mlle Vigée she had studied under Greuze and Carle Vernet; at twenty she married the picture dealer J. B. Le Brun. Her work achieved delicacy and a charmingly impulsive style which is manifestly feminine. She painted several portraits of the queen (cf. fig. 54). One of her most exquisite works is the portrait of Mme Grand (fig. 55), a beautiful English divorcee whose marriage with Talleyrand in 1802 was commanded by Napoleon. When the fury of the Revolution broke, Mme Le Brun prudently withdrew to Naples, where she painted, among others, a portrait of Catherine Skavronska (fig. 56), wife of the Russian ambassador. Soon afterward she moved on to St. Petersburg, where her popularity continued. Members of the Austrian, German, and English aristocracies were also delighted to have her paint them. In her later work she kept abreast of the prevailing mode by hardening her line and texture and to some extent classicizing her composition.

But the mention of Vigée's classical phase carries us ahead of our story. Under the Regency, three quarters of a century earlier, the rococo style, as it is now called, had undergone a rapid evolution. Its lightness of spirit and elaborate ornamentation were immediately embraced by the cultivated minds of France, and were imitated unquestioningly by the courts of Europe generally. But despite all the enthusiasm about it, perhaps because of the enthusiasm, it was destined soon to be thrown ruthlessly into the discard. Even la Pompadour is said to have deplored certain excesses of rocaille ornamentation. Taste can never remain static, and the only direction in which the taste of la Pompadour's time could move was toward simplification. In the middle of the century the excavations at Herculaneum and Pompeii had yielded many objects of Roman and Graeco-Roman art, and Winckelmann's publications soon spread abroad the knowledge of the discoveries. Everything worked together toward the alteration in taste, and the Louis XVI style became far simpler and more delicate than the rococo had been. But the change in the direction of the neoclassic was destined to be far more drastic before it reached its logical conclusion.

It was at this juncture that Jacques Louis David (1748-1825) burst upon the world of art. He had trained under Boucher, and his early portraits were delicately painted in the accepted manner of Louis XVI's time. But as early as the exhibition of 1785 his Oath of the Horatii won over the Parisian public at a blow. It was composed of forms extremely Roman and expressed the loftiest Roman sentiments. Diderot's desire for a moralizing art was realized at last. The new aesthetic attitude swept all before it. The cold austerity and noble gestures of David's new style are brilliantly illustrated in The Death of Socrates, owned by this Museum. Paris and Helen (fig. 57), painted in 1788, shows that the ornament and postures adapted from ancient art could be employed with great distinction and grace. The Bastille had already fallen when the picture was exhibited in the

Salon of 1789. Together with it was shown The Lictors Bringing Back to Brutus the Bodies of His Sons, and David was at once proclaimed the leader of Revolutionary art. He was soon to become its inexorable dictator. In his portraiture we find all the high merit and none of the fatiguing qualities of the historical compositions. His portrait of Mme de Richemont and her daughter (fig. 58), painted at the turn of the century, is completely satisfying. It exhibits in the fullest measure the dignity, purity, and strength which the new style was capable of attaining.

The disgust which arose in France for the art of the monarchy is described by Anatole France[1] in recounting the reminiscences of his elderly friend M. Dubois. Dubois as a youth had been taken to call at the house of Mme de Noailles, where he had seen a complete interior in the latest classical style. He describes it all to Anatole France and adds: "When, on my return home I saw our secretaries with their bulging curves, the armchairs with their twisted feet, the tapestries with their shepherds and their sheep, I almost wept for shame and mortification. I tried to make my father understand that these old-fashioned things were quite ridiculous and that even the Chinese themselves had never produced anything so absurd and grotesque. My father agreed." So in fact did everyone, and it required another complete cycle of taste, aided by the devoted researches of the Goncourt brothers, to bring eighteenth-century art down from the attics!

HARRY B. WEHLE.

[1] The Bloom of Life, pp. 183 ff. New York, 1923.

FRENCH SCULPTURE *OF THE XVIII CENTURY*

In sculpture, as in painting, there was no abrupt transition in France between the style of the late seventeenth century and that of the early eighteenth. The same highly centralized supervision of the arts to the end that they might most effectively serve the king controlled the major part of the activity in both fields during Louis XIV's long reign. The dominating influence of Charles Le Brun, to whom had been entrusted the direction of all the artistic projects of the Crown, made itself everywhere felt. Although by profession a painter, Le Brun did not confine himself to that art alone. He supplied, for instance, many designs for sculpture, which the numerous able sculptors of the day carried out in all humility. Whereas on the whole it cannot be said that his artistic influence was for the good, neither can it be denied that without his coördination much less would have been accomplished. The focal point of aesthetic endeavor in France in the late seventeenth century was the embellishment of the royal châteaux and of their gardens. To this motive we owe much of the significant French art of that time. It is unlikely that it could have been produced without a strong hand in authority at the helm.

Fortunately, there were among the late seventeenth-century sculptors a few men whose creative personalities were virile enough to withstand Le Brun's dictatorship. Of these François Girardon (1628-1715) and Charles Antoine Coysevox (1640-1720) are the most conspicuous. Both men saw their principal activity before the close of the *grand siècle;* both crossed into the new century along with their royal patron, Girardon dying, curiously enough, on the same day as the king, Coysevox a brief five years later. In general their work is not dissimilar, allied as it is through the channels of Roman classicism, of the baroque Italians, and of Le Brun's designs. Girardon's style, however, in its more personal moments possesses a delicacy and sweetness which point the way to the succeeding century. Coyse-

13

vox, the more vigorous personality of the two, rarely forgot the tenets of the grand manner.

Both these sculptors may be best studied at Versailles, where, on the decorations of the château and its gardens, much of their energy was expended. The Fountain of the Pyramid (1670), the Bath of the Nymphs (1670), the Basin of Saturn (1677) are all characteristic of Girardon at the height of his career. His famous Rape of Proserpine (1679) can hardly be regarded as one of his more inspired works, and its indebtedness to Bologna's Rape of the Sabine Women is little less than plagiaristic. He was most successful in his tomb of Cardinal Richelieu (1694) in the church of the Sorbonne in Paris, which is conceived with great dignity and tenderness. Girardon's output after the year 1700 was limited, and he is not represented in the present exhibition. But his influence on the earlier generation of French eighteenth-century sculptors is important.

Coysevox at his best may be regarded as a French counterpart of the Italian Bernini, although he lacked the extraordinary virtuosity that distinguished Bernini's work. He was the sculptor par excellence of Louis XIV's reign, and his garden and fountain sculptures at Versailles seem completely appropriate. Much of his work has a solid, dramatic grandeur edged with pompousness, which renders it peculiarly in harmony with its setting. A long series of portrait busts permitted him to express the realistic side of his talent, which could on occasion attain enviable heights. His powerful portrait of the Grand Condé (1688) must be reckoned among the strongest and most spirited that the century produced. Two of his later portraits, those of the dauphin (fig. 61), executed in 1711, the year of the prince's death, and of Louis XV (fig. 62), done in 1716, when the young king was only six years old, are included in the exhibition. A pair of fine bronzes (figs. 59, 60) illustrate, at reduced scale, the celebrated marble equestrian groups of Fame and Mercury which he completed in 1702 for the gardens of the royal château of Marly. Towards the end of his life Coysevox did not wholly escape the humanizing influence that had put in its appearance, and certain of his later works, notably the

Marie Adélaïde of Savoy as Diana (1710) in the Louvre, give evidence of concession to an increasingly popular naturalism.

Of Girardon's pupils Robert Le Lorrain (1666-1743) was the most eminent. Unfortunately little of his work has survived, but from what is left we can readily understand the respect in which he was universally held by his contemporaries. The most important of his clients were the Rohan family, who employed him in both Paris and Strasbourg. His chef-d'œuvre, the superb relief of the Horses of the Sun, may still be seen over the entrance to the stables of the hôtel de Rohan in Paris. It is one of the most animated and brilliant compositions in all French sculpture, and it is difficult to believe that it was executed well towards the end of the sculptor's career. In the Horses of the Sun the formal rigidity and heaviness of the seventeenth century have been replaced by the direct and spirited naturalism favored by the new era.

Coysevox's two nephews, Nicolas (1658-1733) and Guillaume Coustou (1677-1746), were his outstanding pupils. As the span of their lives would suggest, the old and the new tendencies are combined in their work. Nicolas, the elder of the brothers, adhered more closely to Coysevox's teachings, and his style, although frequently of considerable dignity, is for the most part an echo of his uncle's. His work is essentially seventeenth century in feeling. Guillaume was more impressionable, less bound by tradition. His well-known equestrian groups (1712), executed, like those by Coysevox already mentioned, for the gardens of the château of Marly, show definite strides in the direction of emphasis on nature. His representation of Marie Leczinska as Juno (1731), now in the Louvre, is full of the graceful and intimate charm of the rococo. In the field of portraiture likewise Guillaume abandoned much of the old affectation in favor of realism. The bust in terracotta of his brother Nicolas in the Louvre and that in bronze of the chancelier de Pontchartrain (fig. 63) in the present exhibition are striking instances of truthful characterization.

In Guillaume Coustou's pupil Edme Bouchardon (1698-1762) classicism found a new exponent. His most elaborate undertaking, the monumental fountain (1739-1745) in the rue de Grenelle in Paris, is designed, on the whole, in a restrained, academic manner. The reliefs of the four seasons (figs. 65-68) on this fountain come, therefore, as somewhat of a surprise, for they display all the studied playfulness and informality prescribed in the rococo formula. In fact, these highly mannered sculptures, with their engaging infants absorbed in pseudo-serious occupations, are as thoroughly mid-eighteenth century in feeling as one could want. Another of Bouchardon's widely known sculptures is the Cupid Cutting His Bow from the Club of Hercules, of which a small version (fig. 64) is shown in the exhibition. Here the sculptor is working in the classical tradition fostered by his long sojourn (1723-1732) in Rome. But it is a classicism of a sweet variety in perfect accord with its period and a long way from the robust and vigorous classicism of the preceding century.

There is little doubt that the highest level of achievement in French eighteenth-century sculpture is to be found in the field of portraiture. Such names as Lemoyne, Caffieri, Pigalle, Pajou, and Houdon evoke immediately as thrilling an array of portrait busts as any age can produce. Photography had not put in its appearance, and with the painter as his sole competitor of importance the sculptor found himself in stimulating demand among those who wished to be perpetuated. Jean Baptiste Lemoyne (1704-1778), the earliest of the above group, was the son of Jean Louis Lemoyne (1665-1755), an accomplished sculptor of the late baroque school. Owing perhaps to the fact that circumstances prevented him from making the usual trip to Rome, Lemoyne appears to have more or less escaped the often questionable effects of classical training. Although he was engaged at various times in his career on monumental projects, of which the destroyed statue of Louis XV at Rennes was the most important, it is his remarkable and very personal series of portrait busts for which he is remembered. His poignant and direct style may be seen at its best in his brilliant likeness of the maréchal d'Harcourt (fig. 70), which leaves little to be desired in the way of shrewd and penetrating insight.

Lemoyne had a number of talented pupils, among them Pigalle,

Falconet, and Pajou—a fortunate circumstance for posterity, but not for Lemoyne himself, whose reputation as a result suffered something of an eclipse. Jean Baptiste Pigalle (1714-1785) was a versatile sculptor whose standing in his day was aided by Mme de Pompadour's favor. His repertory included idealistic and religious groups, tombs, and portraits, not to mention ventures in the field of child anatomy, exemplified in a series of putti, the Child with a Cage (fig. 75) being the best known. Of his idealistic sculptures the most successful was the Mercury Fastening His Sandals (fig. 74), a marble of which was presented by Louis XV to Frederick the Great. The lithe grace and easy, though complex, posture of this figure combine to make it an outstanding work of its period. The statues of the Virgin in the churches of Saint Eustache (1748) and Saint Sulpice (1774) are executed in an ingratiating rococo vein. It was on his sepulchral monuments that the strength and inventiveness of Pigalle's genius found its proper outlet. The tomb of the maréchal de Saxe in the church of Saint Thomas at Strasbourg is a truly masterly composition. Pigalle's portraits (cf. fig. 76) display a masculine realism almost completely free of affectation.

Pigalle's brother-in-law, Gabriel Christophe Allegrain (1710-1795), was a sculptor of no mean ability, who is less widely recognized today than many of his contemporaries, owing to the fact that his extant works are not numerous. Allegrain's two best-known sculptures are his marbles of Diana and Venus at their baths, now in the Louvre. That of Venus (fig. 73), the finer of the two, was ordered for the king in 1755. It was completed twelve years later and given to Mme du Barry, who placed it in her gardens at Louveciennes. A very graceful figure it is, ingeniously posed and replete with the charm of its period.

As in painting the eighteenth century saw the increased importance of the small, so-called easel picture, in sculpture it witnessed a comparable change in favor of the statuette. Thus a man like Étienne Maurice Falconet (1716-1791) is perhaps best known today not for his monumental works but for his diminutive groups in marble and *biscuit de Sèvres.* Unrivaled in their delicacy and thoroughly rococo prettiness, these little sculptures (figs. 77-81) constitute the perfect type of ornament for the drawing-room and boudoir. Falconet's svelte and impersonal style is well illustrated in his famous Nymph Descending to Her Bath (1757), of which a small terracotta (fig. 82) may be seen in the exhibition. It would be difficult to imagine a figure more utterly French, more completely in accord with its epoch.

One of the finest series of portrait sculptures to be found anywhere in France today is the property of that venerable and extraordinary institution, the Comédie Française. Comprised, for the most part, of likenesses of literary and theatrical celebrities, this collection includes splendid examples of the work of such men as Lemoyne, Caffieri, Pajou, and Houdon. Jean Jacques Caffieri (1725-1792), especially, may be studied to good advantage in the Comédie Française, and we are fortunate, therefore, in having been able to borrow his busts of Belloy (fig. 86) and Rotrou (fig. 88) for the exhibition. He was the most distinguished of a long line of sculptors, of which the founder, Filippo, came to Paris from Rome in 1660. Jean Jacques's portraits, on which his reputation principally depends, were often characterized by vibrant intenseness combined with a certain stylish idealization. He was on occasion very successful in his handling of the difficult problem of posthumous portraiture. The busts of Rotrou and of the maréchal du Muy (fig. 87) fall in that category. In quite a different vein is a symbolic statuette of Hope Nourishing Love (fig. 85) designed in a highly postured but none the less pleasing manner.

The lives of all the sculptors to whom reference has so far been made fall within the seventeenth and eighteenth centuries. We now come to a group whose lives—and even in some cases whose periods of activity—extend into the nineteenth. They may be regarded collectively as the later generation of French eighteenth-century sculptors. In their work is to be found not only the culmination of the rococo tradition of the full eighteenth century but also, to a more limited degree, the literal and academic classicism which became increasingly the fashion as the end of the century approached. The earliest of this group was Augustin Pajou (1730-1809), who, we have already noted, was one of Lemoyne's most talented pupils. His energies were divided among decorative compositions, of which those in the *Salle de l'Opéra* at Versailles are the most important, symbolic and allegorical subjects, and portraiture. His reputation was already well established when in 1770 he was asked by Mme du Barry to do her portrait. Her marble bust in the Louvre, probably the most widely known sculptured portrait of the entire eighteenth century, was the result. In his likenesses of women Pajou was apt to err on the side of prettiness, but he occasionally transcended this tendency and arrived at true distinction, as, for instance, in his admirable bust of Mme de Wailly (fig. 95).

Claude Michel (1738-1814), better known as Clodion, perhaps the most facile and certainly the most animated sculptor that the French eighteenth century produced, was Pajou's son-in-law. Born in Nancy, Clodion went to Paris at the age of seventeen. There he studied with his uncle, Lambert Sigisbert Adam, and Pigalle, afterwards spending nine years in Rome. For some curious reason classicism made no deep impression on him, and he developed the most rococo of styles at a time when the rococo was already outmoded and classicism the established vogue. Nymphs (cf. figs. 102, 103), satyrs, and bacchanalian subjects (cf. fig. 100) were among his favorite themes and were often carried out in terracotta, a medium over which he had an unrivaled command. Clodion's style is frequently characterized by excited movement and occasionally by touches of mild sensuality. In no sculptor's work is to be found more of the joy of living, and this may be one reason why Clodion's sculptures have always enjoyed wide popularity.

There is little doubt, everything considered, that the greatest sculptor of the eighteenth century in France was Jean Antoine Houdon (1741-1828). His finest work, the seated Voltaire (1781) of the Comédie Française, is surely one of the chefs-d'œuvre of all time. His long series of portrait busts forms an authentic record of the society of the day unparalleled in the history of sculpture. Houdon possessed an almost psychic capacity for discerning the essential characters of his subjects and a genius for transferring his perceptions to clay. He was equally happy in his portraits of men and women, of adults and children. His piercing style may be observed to advantage in such likenesses as those of Franklin (fig. 109), Mme de Thélusson (fig. 114), the youthful Alexandre Brongniart (fig. 104), and the infant Sabine (fig. 113). In comparison with his portraits, Houdon's numerous ventures in the field of idealistic and decorative sculpture are less consequential. But this test is unjustifiably severe, for on occasion, as in the superb figures of Diana (1780) formerly in the Hermitage and The Bather (fig. 110) in this Museum, he attained distinction of a high order. Of all the French eighteenth-century sculptors Houdon is the best known in America, for it was he who did a number of excellent portraits of public characters of the post-Revolutionary period, of which the full-length marble figure of Washington (1792) in the Virginia State Capitol is the most notable.

Whereas the sculptors we have mentioned were the principal contributors to the development of sculptural style in France in the eighteenth century, there were in addition numerous artists of established reputation whose work on occasion approaches in quality that of the more celebrated. Thus the various members of the Adam and Slodtz families, and such men as Mouchy, Vassé, Defernex, Monot, Marin, Boizot, and Chinard frequently displayed enviable talent. But on the whole they merge into the stylistic current without changing its direction or modifying its character. Joseph Chinard (1756-1813) of Lyon did, however, in his later years develop a personal style which stamps him as the most representative French sculptor of the Napoleonic period. His sympathetic portrait of Mme Récamier (fig. 118), whose friend he was, reflects accurately, in its decorative stylization, the temper of the new era.

PRESTON REMINGTON.

ILLUSTRATIONS

1   NICOLAS DE LARGILLIÈRE, 1656-1746
LE COMTE DE PUYSÉGUR
Canvas. H. 53½ in.; W. 41¼ in.
             Lent by Mrs. Marjorie Post Hutton

2   NICOLAS DE LARGILLIÈRE
LE MARQUIS DE MONTESPAN
Canvas. H. 53 in.; w. 41 in.   Signed: Peint. par. N/De. Largillierre. 1710.
Lent by the California Palace of the Legion of Honor

3   JEAN ANTOINE WATTEAU, 1684-1721

ITALIAN SERENADE. Originally owned by Titon de Tillet, maître d'hôtel to Marie Adélaïde, mother of Louis XV. Subsequently in the collection of Watteau's friend Jean de Jullienne.

Panel. H. 14⅛ in.; w. 11 in.

Lent by the Estate of John R. Thompson

4   JEAN ANTOINE WATTEAU

JUPITER AND ANTIOPE. Formerly in the Patureau Collection. The composition appears as a statue in Watteau's Champs Élysées, now in the Wallace Collection.

Canvas. H. 28¾ in.; w. 42⅛ in.

Lent by the Musée du Louvre (Donation La Caze)

5   JEAN ANTOINE WATTEAU

LE MEZZETIN. This painting was bought from the artist by his friend Jean de Jullienne. Later it was acquired by Catherine the Great of Russia; subsequently it passed into the collection of the Hermitage.

Canvas. H. 21¾ in.; w. 17 in.

From the collection of The Metropolitan Museum of Art
Frank A. Munsey Fund

6   JEAN BAPTISTE JOSEPH PATER, 1695-1736

TROOPS ON THE MARCH. Formerly in the collections of Baron Adolphe de Rothschild and Baron Maurice de Rothschild.

Canvas. H. 21¼ in.; w. 25¾ in.

Lent by Mrs. Julian Humphreys

7   JEAN BAPTISTE JOSEPH PATER

TROOPS AT REST. Formerly in the collections of Baron Adolphe de Rothschild and Baron Maurice de Rothschild.

Canvas. H. 21¼ in.; w. 25¾ in.

                Lent by Mrs. Julian Humphreys

8   JEAN BAPTISTE JOSEPH PATER

LADIES BATHING, WITH STATUE OF VENUS. Formerly in the collection of Rodolphe Kann.

Canvas. H. 19⅞ in.; W. 23⅞ in.

                         Lent by J. P. Morgan

9   JEAN BAPTISTE JOSEPH PATER

LADIES BATHING, WITH FIGURE OF NEPTUNE. Formerly in the
collection of Rodolphe Kann.
Canvas. H. 19⅞ in.; W. 23⅞ in.
                    Lent by J. P. Morgan

10   JEAN BAPTISTE JOSEPH PATER

THE SWING. Formerly in the Holford Collection.

Canvas. H. 18 in.; W. 21⅜ in.

                        Lent by Emil J. Stehli

11   NICOLAS LANCRET, 1690-1743

MLLE CAMARGO DANCING. (Marie Anne de Cuppi de Camargo, a popular dancer in the Opéra.) Painted about 1730. Formerly in the collection of Frederick II of Prussia at Potsdam.

Canvas. H. 30 in.; W. 41¾ in.

Lent by Andrew W. Mellon

12   NICOLAS LANCRET

THE HAM LUNCH (*Le Déjeuner de jambon*). A small sketch for or replica of the painting, now in the Musée Condé, ordered in 1735 by Louis XV for the dining room of the *petits appartements* at Versailles, as a pendant to Le Déjeuner d'huîtres by De Troy.

Canvas. H. 21¼ in.; W. 17¾ in.

Lent by D. David-Weill

13   NICOLAS LANCRET

NICAISE. One of a series of illustrations for the *Contes* of La Fontaine. Formerly
in the Radziwill and Beurnonville Collections.
Copper. H. 11¼ in.; w. 14 in.

Lent by J. P. Morgan

14   NICOLAS LANCRET

THE TWO FRIENDS (*Les Deux Amis*). One of a series of illustrations for the *Contes* of La Fontaine. Exhibited in the Salon of 1739.
Copper. H. 11 in.; W. 14 in.

                              Lent by J. P. Morgan

15   NICOLAS LANCRET

THE DUET. Formerly in the collection of Sir William Knighton.
Canvas. H. 19¾ in.; w. 16½ in.

Lent by Emil J. Stehli

16   JEAN MARC NATTIER, 1685-1766

MME MARSOLLIER AND HER DAUGHTER. Formerly in the Porgès Collection.

Canvas. H. 57½ in.; w. 45 in.   Signed: Nattier pinxit/1749.

          Lent by Mrs. Robert W. Schuette

17 JEAN MARC NATTIER

*LOUISE ÉLISABETH, DUCHESSE DE PARME, AND HER DAUGH-
TER ISABELLE.* A portrait of the eldest daughter of Louis XV painted for her
husband, the infante Philip, son of Philip V of Spain.

Canvas. H. 52½ in.; w. 42 in. Signed: Nattier. Pinxit/1750.

Lent by Mrs. Marjorie Post Hutton

18   JEAN MARC NATTIER

MME DE LAPORTE (NÉE CAUMARTIN) AS FLORA

Canvas. H. 40¼ in.; w. 32⅛ in.   Signed: Nattier. pinxit/1752

Inscribed: M^M de Caumartin femme de/M de La Porte conseiller d'etat/1759

Lent by James Speyer

19   JEAN MARC NATTIER

MME HENRIETTE PLAYING THE VIOLONCELLO. A posthumous
portrait of the second daughter of Louis XV.

Canvas. H. 92⅛ in.; w. 64¼ in.   Signed: Nattier pinxit/1754

Lent by the Musée de Versailles

20   JEAN BAPTISTE SIMÉON CHARDIN, 1699-1779

THE YOUNG SOLDIER. Exhibited in the Salon of 1737.

Panel. H. 8½ in.; w. 7⅛ in.   Signed: Chardin

Lent by Baron Henri de Rothschild

21   JEAN BAPTISTE SIMÉON CHARDIN

LITTLE GIRL WITH CHERRIES. Exhibited in the Salon of 1737.
Panel. H. 8 in.; W. 7 in.

Lent by Baron Henri de Rothschild

22   JEAN BAPTISTE SIMÉON CHARDIN

GRACE BEFORE MEAT (*Le Bénédicité*). An earlier version of this subject, belonging also to the Louvre, was exhibited in the Salon of 1740. Several other repetitions exist.

Canvas. H. 19¼ in.; w. 15⅜ in.

            Lent by the Musée du Louvre (Donation La Caze)

23   JEAN BAPTISTE SIMÉON CHARDIN

THE WHITE TEAPOT

Canvas. H. 12½ in.; w. 15¾ in.   Signed: Chardin./1764

Lent by the Museum of Fine Arts, Boston

24   JEAN BAPTISTE SIMÉON CHARDIN

THE HARE

Canvas. H. 25½ in.; W. 32 in.   Signed: Chardin

Lent by Henry P. McIlhenny

25   JEAN BAPTISTE SIMÉON CHARDIN

APPLES, PEAR, AND WHITE MUG

Canvas. H. 13 in.; w. 16⅛ in.

Lent by Mrs. William R. Timken

26   JEAN BAPTISTE SIMÉON CHARDIN

MME CHARDIN (NÉE POUGET). A replica of the pastel in the Louvre dated 1775.

Pastel. H. 17⅞ in.; w. 14½ in.   Signed: Chardin 1776

Lent by Forsyth Wickes

27   FRANÇOIS BOUCHER, 1703-1770

YOUNG WOMAN WITH A MUFF

Cardboard. H. 25¼ in.; w. 20⅞ in.

       Lent by the Musée du Louvre (Donation La Caze)

28   FRANÇOIS BOUCHER

DIANA'S RETURN FROM THE HUNT. The pendant to this painting, Les
Confidences pastorales, is in the collection of Prince Jacques de Broglie.
Canvas. H. 36¾ in.; w. 52 in.   Signed: f · Boucher · 1745 ·
                        Lent by the Musée Cognacq-Jay

29   FRANÇOIS BOUCHER

THE TWO CONFIDANTES. Formerly in the collections of Mme de Pompadour and her brother, the marquis de Marigny.

Canvas. H. 32½ in.; w. 29½ in.   Signed: · f· Boucher/1750

Lent by Mrs. William R. Timken

30   FRANÇOIS BOUCHER

THE TOILET OF VENUS. Painted for Mme de Pompadour, this picture
later came into the possession of her brother, the marquis de Marigny; subsequently it was in the collection of the comte de la Beraudìete.

Canvas. H. 42⅝ in.; w. 33½ in.   Signed: f · Boucher—1751

From the collection of The Metropolitan Museum of Art
Bequest of William K. Vanderbilt

31   JEAN BAPTISTE GREUZE, 1725-1805

INDOLENCE (*La Paresseuse*). Probably painted in Rome. Exhibited as La Paresseuse italienne in the Salon of 1757, lent by Boyer de Fonscolombe. Canvas. H. 25¼ in.; w. 19½ in.

Lent by the Wadsworth Atheneum

32   JEAN BAPTISTE GREUZE

THE BROKEN EGGS (*Les Œufs cassés*). Formerly in the collections of Prince Anatole Demidoff and Sir Richard Wallace.

Canvas. H. 28¾ in.; W. 37 in.   Signed: Greuze f. Roma 1756

From the collection of The Metropolitan Museum of Art
Bequest of William K. Vanderbilt

33   JEAN BAPTISTE GREUZE

GIRL WINDING YARN (*La Dévideuse*). Exhibited in the Salon of 1759, lent by the marquis de Blondel. It later belonged to La Live de Jully, the duc de Choiseul, the duc de Morny, and Sir Richard Wallace.

Canvas. H. 29½ in.; w. 24¼ in.

Lent by J. P. Morgan

34   JEAN BAPTISTE GREUZE

THE DEAD BIRD. Exhibited in the Salon of 1800.
Panel. H. 26¾ in.; w. 21⅝ in.

                       Lent by the Musée du Louvre

35   JEAN BAPTISTE GREUZE

LE COMTE D'ANGIVILLER. (Director of the Crown Buildings.) A replica
of this portrait is in the Musée de Metz.

Canvas. H. 25¼ in.; W. 21¼ in.

Lent by Albert Blum

36   JEAN BAPTISTE GREUZE

JEAN JACQUES CAFFIERI. A portrait of the sculptor. Formerly in the Doucet Collection.

Canvas. H. 25¼ in.; W. 20¾ in.

Lent by Mrs. Julian Humphreys

37   JEAN BAPTISTE GREUZE

THE FIRST LESSON IN LOVE

Canvas. H. 15⅝ in.; W. 12¾ in.

Lent by Emil J. Stehli

38   JEAN BAPTISTE PERRONNEAU, 1715-1783

LA DUCHESSE D'AYEN. Formerly in the collection of the sister of the
duchesse d'Ayen, from whose descendants it was acquired by the present owner.
Canvas. H. 47¼ in.; w. 39⅜ in.   Signed: Perronneau 1748

Lent by D. David-Weill

39   CHARLES AMÉDÉE PHILIPPE VAN LOO, 1719-1795

THE SOAP BUBBLES. Formerly in the Hohenzollern Collection, Charlottenburg. Portraits of the artist's children.

Canvas. H. 34¾ in.; w. 34¾ in.   Signed: Amédée . Van Loo./1764.

Lent by Mrs. Robert W. Schuette

40   CHARLES AMÉDÉE PHILIPPE VAN LOO

THE MAGIC LANTERN. Formerly in the Hohenzollern Collection, Charlottenburg. Portraits of the artist's children.

Canvas. H. 34¾ in.; w. 34¾ in.   Signed: Amédée Van Loo/1764

Lent by Mrs. Robert W. Schuette

41   FRANÇOIS HUBERT DROUAIS, 1727-1775

PORTRAIT OF A GIRL

Canvas. H. 21½ in.; W. 18 in.   Signed: Drouais/1761

Lent by Mr. and Mrs. Charles V. Hickox

42   FRANÇOIS HUBERT DROUAIS

BOY WITH A HAT

Canvas. H. 25¾ in.; w. 21½ in.

Lent by Albert Blum

43   FRANÇOIS HUBERT DROUAIS

MARIE ANTOINETTE, DAUPHINE. Painted between 1770 and 1774.
Canvas. H. 25½ in.; W. 21½ in.

Lent by Count Allard du Chollet

44   JEAN HONORÉ FRAGONARD, 1732-1806

THE BATHERS. Sold from the collection of Varanchan de Saint-Geniès in 1777.

Canvas. H. 25¼ in.; w. 31½ in.

       Lent by the Musée du Louvre (Donation La Caze)

45   JEAN HONORÉ FRAGONARD

THE READER. Sold from the Senneville Collection in 1780 and from the Cronier Collection in 1905.

Canvas. H. 32¼ in.; W. 25⅝ in.

Lent anonymously

NOTE

Item Number 45, The Reader, by Jean Honoré Fragonard, lent anonymously to the Exhibition of French Painting and Sculpture of the XVIII Century until December 6, 1935, has been replaced by the Self-Portrait by Élisabeth Louise Vigée Le Brun, lent by Mrs. Henry J. Pierce.

46   JEAN HONORÉ FRAGONARD

THE LOVE LETTER (*Le Billet Doux*). A portrait of Boucher's daughter, Marie Émilie, who married in 1773 Charles Étienne Gabriel Cuvillier, one of the king's architects, to whom the letter is addressed. Formerly in the Cronier and Bardac Collections.

Canvas. H. 32 in.; W. 26 in.

Lent by Jules S. Bache

47   JEAN HONORÉ FRAGONARD

LOVE (*L'Amour*). L'Amour and La Folie were subjects repeated by Fragonard and frequently copied and engraved by others. This painting and its pendant (No. 48) are the finest examples of the famous pair.

Canvas. H. 22 in.; W. 18½ in.   Signed: frago

Lent by Andrew W. Mellon

48   JEAN HONORÉ FRAGONARD

FOLLY (La Folie).

Canvas. H. 22 in.; w. 18½ in.   Signed: frago

Lent by Andrew W. Mellon

49   JEAN HONORÉ FRAGONARD

THE HAPPY FAMILY (*L'Heureuse Fécondité*)

Canvas. H. 21¼ in.; W. 25½ in.

Lent by Mrs. William R. Timken

50   HUBERT ROBERT, 1733-1808

THE PORTICO OF A COUNTRY MANSION. Exhibited in the Salon of 1775 from the collection of M. de Frouville.

Canvas. H. 80¾ in.; W. 48¼ in. Signed: H ·/ Robert ·/ PINXIT · L ·/ PARISORUM/ ANNO 1773

From the collection of The Metropolitan Museum of Art
Bequest of Lucy Work Hewitt

51   HUBERT ROBERT

THE RETURN OF THE CATTLE. Exhibited in the Salon of 1775 from the collection of M. de Frouville.

Canvas. H. 80¾ in.; w. 48¼ in.

From the collection of The Metropolitan Museum of Art
Bequest of Lucy Work Hewitt

52   HUBERT ROBERT

THE FLOOD

Canvas. H. 19¾ in.; W. 15¾ in.

Lent by James Speyer

Photograph, William Rockhill Nelson Gallery of Art

53   HUBERT ROBERT

TERRACE OF THE CHÂTEAU DE MARLY

Canvas. H. 35½ in.; W. 52 in.

Lent by the William Rockhill Nelson Gallery of Art

54   ÉLISABETH LOUISE VIGÉE LE BRUN, 1755-1842

MARIE ANTOINETTE. In a letter to the prince de Beauffremont, former owner of this portrait, Vigée Le Brun refers to it as painted in 1778.
Canvas. H. 36½ in.; W. 29½ in.

Lent by Edward J. Berwind

55   ÉLISABETH LOUISE VIGÉE LE BRUN

MME GRAND, LATER PRINCESSE DE TALLEYRAND. Formerly in the Doucet Collection.

Canvas. H. 36¼ in.; w. 28½ in.   Signed: L. E. Le Brun 1783

Lent by Edward S. Harkness

56   ÉLISABETH LOUISE VIGÉE LE BRUN

COUNTESS SKAVRONSKA. (A niece of Potemkin and wife of the Russian ambassador to Naples.) Painted in Naples.

Canvas. H. 31½ in.; w. 26 in. Signed: E . . . Vigée Le Brun/ St petersbourg/ 1790

Lent by Albert Blum

57   JACQUES LOUIS DAVID, 1748-1825

PARIS AND HELEN. Painted by order of the comte d'Artois, later Charles X.
The scene is laid in the Salle des Cariatides of the Louvre.
Canvas. H. 57⅞ in.; W. 70⅞ in.   Signed: L. David faciebat/Parisis anno/
MDCCLXXXVIII

Lent by the Musée du Louvre

58   JACQUES LOUIS DAVID

JEANNE, COMTESSE DE RICHEMONT, AND HER DAUGHTER CAMILLE. Painted about 1800-1802. Formerly in the Bardac and Chabert Collections.

Canvas. H. 45¾ in.; w. 35½ in.

      Lent by Edward J. Berwind

59   CHARLES ANTOINE COYSEVOX, 1640-1720

FAME MOUNTED ON PEGASUS. Small version of the marble group completed in 1702 for Louis XIV for the gardens of the château of Marly. Bronze. H. 30 in.

Lent by Dr. Preston Pope Satterwhite

60   CHARLES ANTOINE COYSEVOX

MERCURY MOUNTED ON PEGASUS. Small version of the marble group
completed in 1702 for Louis XIV for the gardens of the château of Marly.
Bronze. H. 31½ in.

Lent by Dr. Preston Pope Satterwhite

61   CHARLES ANTOINE COYSEVOX

LOUIS DE FRANCE, GRAND DAUPHIN. (1661-1711; eldest son of Louis XIV.) Formerly in the marquis d'Osmond and Rikoff Collections. Bronze. H. 35 in.   Executed about 1711

Lent by George Blumenthal

62   CHARLES ANTOINE COYSEVOX

LOUIS XV. (1710-1774.)   The king at six years of age.

Marble. H. 25½ in.   Executed in 1716.   Signed: · A · COYZEUOX ·

Lent by Baron Maurice de Rothschild

63   GUILLAUME COUSTOU, 1677-1746

LE CHANCELIER DE PONTCHARTRAIN. (1643-1727; Louis Phelypeaux, comte de Pontchartrain.) Formerly in the collection of the marquise d'Avrincourt. Bronze. H. 26¾ in.   Signed: G · COVSTOV · FECIT · ANNO · 1727 ·

Lent by D. David-Weill

64   EDME BOUCHARDON, 1698-1762

CUPID CUTTING HIS BOW FROM THE CLUB OF HERCULES. From the collections of the Marquis of Hertford, Sir Richard Wallace, and Sir John Murray Scott.

Marble. H. 29¾ in.   Signed: BOUCHARDON 1744.

Lent by John M. Schiff

65, 66   EDME BOUCHARDON

SPRING, SUMMER. Reduced versions of the reliefs on the fountain, completed in 1745, in the rue de Grenelle, Paris.

Marble. Each: H. 20¼ in.; W. 33¾ in.

From the collection of The Metropolitan Museum of Art

Harris Brisbane Dick Fund

67, 68   EDME BOUCHARDON

AUTUMN, WINTER. Reduced versions of the reliefs on the fountain, completed in 1745, in the rue de Grenelle, Paris.

Marble. Each: H. 20¼ in.; W. 33¾ in.

From the collection of The Metropolitan Museum of Art
Joseph Pulitzer Bequest, 1935

69   JEAN BAPTISTE LEMOYNE, 1704-1778

LOUIS XV. (1710-1774.) Presented by the king to Mme de Pompadour. Subsequently in the collection of the marquis de la Briffe.

Marble. H. 34 in.   Signed: *par/J · B · Lemoyne/*1757

Lent by George Blumenthal

70   JEAN BAPTISTE LEMOYNE

LE MARÉCHAL D'HARCOURT. (1701-1783; Anne Pierre, duc d'Harcourt.)
Terracotta. H. 26 in.   Executed about 1760
Lent by Mrs. John D. Rockefeller, Jr.

71   JEAN BAPTISTE LEMOYNE

MME DE LA POPELINIÈRE. (Second wife of Alexandre Jean Joseph Le Riche de la Popelinière, financier.)

Marble. H. 30 in.   Signed: *par/J. B. Lemoyne/*1769

Lent by Mrs. Alexander Hamilton Rice

72   JEAN BAPTISTE LEMOYNE

LA DUCHESSE DE LA ROCHEFOUCAULD. (Born 1745; Félicité Sophie de Lannion.)

Marble. H. 28¾ in.   Signed: *par/J · B · Lemoyne/*1774

From the collection of The Metropolitan Museum of Art

Mr. and Mrs. Isaac D. Fletcher Fund

73   GABRIEL CHRISTOPHE ALLEGRAIN, 1710-1795

VENUS AT HER BATH. Presented by Louis XV to Mme du Barry in 1772 for her gardens at Louveciennes.

Marble. H. 68⅞ in. Executed in 1767.   Signed: G · C · ALLEGRAIN · FECIT/ · 1767 ·

Lent by the Musée du Louvre

74   JEAN BAPTISTE PIGALLE, 1714-1785

MERCURY FASTENING HIS SANDALS

Terracotta. H. 22 in. Executed in Rome between 1736 and 1739; *morceau 'de réception à l'Académie* in 1741.

From the collection of The Metropolitan Museum of Art
Bequest of Benjamin Altman

75   JEAN BAPTISTE PIGALLE

CHILD WITH A CAGE. Formerly in the collection of Lily, Duchess of Marlborough.

Bronze. H. 19 in.   Signed: PIGALLE: F./1749

Lent by Mrs. Alexander Hamilton Rice

76 JEAN BAPTISTE PIGALLE

MAJOR GUÉRIN. (1710-1791; surgeon in chief of the armies of the king.)
Bronze. H. 29½ in. Executed between 1775 and 1780
Lent by the Musée du Louvre

77   ÉTIENNE MAURICE FALCONET, 1716-1791

VENUS AND CUPID. Formerly in the collections of Baroness Mathilde de Rothschild and George Blumenthal.

Marble. H. 16 in.

Lent by Henri Étienne Destrem

78   ÉTIENNE MAURICE FALCONET

SEATED WOMAN

Marble. H. 10¼ in.

     Lent by the Musée Cognacq-Jay

79   ÉTIENNE MAURICE FALCONET

WOMAN AND CHILD

Marble. H. 15 in.

Lent by Mrs. Marjorie Post Hutton

80, 81   ÉTIENNE MAURICE FALCONET

VENUS AND CUPID. Formerly in the Morgan and Gary Collections.
Marble. Each: H. 18½ in.

Lent by the Museum of Fine Arts, Boston

82   ÉTIENNE MAURICE FALCONET

NYMPH DESCENDING TO HER BATH. A small version of the marble in
the Louvre.
Terracotta. H. 14⅞ in.

        Lent by Mrs. Frank Gray Griswold

83, 84   ÉTIENNE MAURICE FALCONET

TORCHÈRES. Maidens carrying cornucopias.

Plaster. Each: H. 66 in.

From the collection of Therese K. and Herbert N. Straus

85   JEAN JACQUES CAFFIERI, 1725-1792

HOPE NOURISHING LOVE

Marble. H. 28½ in.   Signed: J · J · CAFFIERI · INVENIT & SCULPSIT · 1769·

Lent by Princess de Faucigny-Lucinge

Photograph, Giraudon

86   JEAN JACQUES CAFFIERI

PIERRE LAURENT BUIRETTE DE BELLOY. (1727-1775; dramatic poet.) The model for this bust was executed in 1765.

Marble. H. 35¾ in.   Signed: *Fait Par Son Ami* CAFFIERI/*En* 1771.

Lent by the Comédie Française

87   JEAN JACQUES CAFFIERI

LE MARÉCHAL DU MUY. (1711-1775; Louis Nicolas Victor, comte du Muy.)

Marble. H. 31½ in.   Signed: I · I · CAFFIERI · SCVLPSIT/1776

From the collection of The Metropolitan Museum of Art

Mr. and Mrs. Isaac D. Fletcher Fund

Photograph, Giraudon

88   JEAN JACQUES CAFFIERI

JEAN DE ROTROU. (1609-1650; dramatic poet.)

Marble. H. 37⅜ in.   Signed: *Fait par* J J CAFFIERI *en*/1783

Lent by the Comédie Française

89   AUGUSTIN PAJOU, 1730–1809

LOUIS, DAUPHIN DE FRANCE. (1729-1765; eldest son of Louis XV.)

Marble. H. 31½ in.   Executed about 1769

Lent by the Musée de Versailles

90   AUGUSTIN PAJOU

SATYR AND CHILD. Formerly in the Kann and Salomon Collections.
Marble. H. 14⅝ in.   Signed: *Pajou. fe.* 1772
                Lent by Mrs. Elisha Walker

91   AUGUSTIN PAJOU

SATYRESS AND CHILD. Formerly in the Kann and Salomon Collections.
Marble. H. 14¼ in.   Signed: *Pajou. fe.* 1772.
             Lent by Mrs. Elisha Walker

92   AUGUSTIN PAJOU

BUFFON. (1707-1788; Georges Louis Leclerc, comte de Buffon; naturalist.)
Marble. H. 28¾ in.   Signed: PAR/PAJOU. SCUL/DV/ROY./ . . . MDCCLXXIII.
Lent by the Musée du Louvre

93   AUGUSTIN PAJOU

BACCHANTE. A small version of the group in the Louvre.

Terracotta. H. 23 ⅞ in.   Signed: *Pajou fct*/1774.

         Lent by Miss Caroline L. Morgan

94   AUGUSTIN PAJOU

MME VIGÉE LE BRUN. (1755-1842; Élisabeth Louise Vigée Le Brun; painter.) Formerly in the Wilbrod Chabrol Collection.

Terracotta. H. 26¼ in.   Signed: *Pajou fc.* 1783.

Lent by Edward J. Berwind

95   AUGUSTIN PAJOU

MME DE WAILLY. (Wife of the court architect Charles de Wailly.) Formerly
in the Lelong, Wagram, David-Weill, and Salomon Collections.
Marble. H. 29¾ in.   Signed: PAJOU. F. 1789.
            Lent by the Estate of Mrs. J. Horace Harding

96   AUGUSTIN PAJOU

PSYCHE ABANDONED

Terracotta. H. 17 in.   Signed: PAR LE CITOYEN/PAJOU,/*L'an* 5*em de La-*/
Republique-/*française.*/1796. *V.*/*Stile*

Lent by John M. Schiff

97   MARTIN CLAUDE MONOT, 1733-1803

LE COMTE DE SÉGUR. (1753-1830; Louis Philippe; soldier, diplomat.)

Marble. H. 26⅜ in.   Executed about 1783

Lent by the Musée de Versailles

Photograph, J. E. Bulloz

98   MARTIN CLAUDE MONOT

LA COMTESSE DE SÉGUR. (1756-1828; née d'Aguesseau, wife of Comte Louis Philippe.)

Marble. H. 26⅜ in.   Executed about 1783

Lent by the Musée de Versailles

99　　　CLAUDE MICHEL, CALLED CLODION, 1738-1814

VASE WITH SACRIFICIAL SCENE

Marble. H. 14¼ in.　　　Signed: CLODION · MIC . . . *invenit et fe . . . in Roma* 1766

Lent by George Blumenthal

100   CLAUDE MICHEL, CALLED CLODION

BACCHANTE

Terracotta. H. 20⅜ in.   Inscribed: CLODION./1798.

Lent by George Blumenthal

101   CLAUDE MICHEL, CALLED CLODION

CUPID RIDING A DOG. Formerly in the Kraemer Collection.

Terracotta. H. 10½ in.   Signed: CLODION./1799.

Lent by John M. Schiff

102, 103   CLAUDE MICHEL, CALLED CLODION

GIRL CARRYING A CHILD. Formerly in the collection of the comtesse de
Montesquiou-Fezensac.

Terracotta. Left, H. 16¼ in. Right, H. 17 in.   Each signed: CLODION.

From the collection of Therese K. and Herbert N. Straus

Photograph, Frick Art Reference Library

104   JEAN ANTOINE HOUDON, 1741-1828

ALEXANDRE BRONGNIART. Formerly in the Bardac Collection.

Marble. H. 14⅞ in.   Signed: A. HOUDON, F. AN. 1777.

Lent by Joseph E. Widener

J. BAPT. POQUELIN - MOLIERE.

105   JEAN ANTOINE HOUDON

MOLIÈRE. (1622-1673; Jean Baptiste Poquelin.) A replica of the marble in the
Comédie Française.

Terracotta. H. 29 in.   Signed: *houdon f.* 1778

Lent by Miss Caroline L. Morgan

112   JEAN ANTOINE HOUDON

VESTAL. Made for the staircase of the hôtel d'Aumont, Paris.
Marble. H. 64 in.   Signed: *houdon f · 1787*
                      Lent by J. P. Morgan

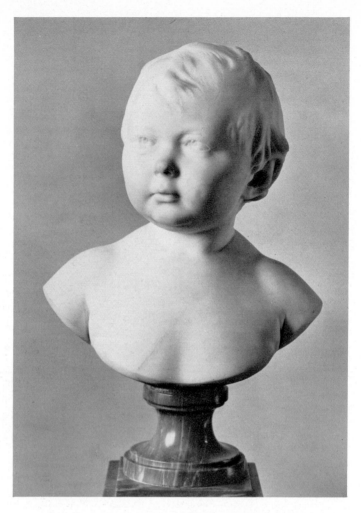

113   JEAN ANTOINE HOUDON

SABINE. (The sculptor's daughter.) For many years in the possession of Mlle Sabine Houdon, afterwards Mme Henri Duval, and her family. Subsequently in the Doucet and Gary Collections.

Marble. H. 17½ in.   Inscribed: *Sabinet houdon,*/1788

Lent by Edward S. Harkness

114   JEAN ANTOINE HOUDON

MME DE THÉLUSSON. (La comtesse de Thélusson de Sorcy, née Rilliet.)

Bronze. H. 33½ in.   Signed: *houdon. f.*/1791

Lent by Mme Jacques Balsan

115   JEAN ANTOINE HOUDON

A YOUNG NAVAL OFFICER

Terracotta. H. 27 in.

                        Lent by J. P. Morgan

116   SIMON LOUIS BOIZOT, 1743-1809

JOSEPH VERNET. (1714-1789; painter.)

Marble. H. 26 in.   Inscribed: *modelé d'après nature en* 1783./*par Boizot, et exécuté en* 1806.

Lent by the Musée du Louvre

117   JOSEPH CHARLES MARIN, 1759-1834

MATERNITY

Terracotta. H. 14¼ in.   Executed about 1795.   Signed: *Marin*

Lent by John M. Schiff

118   JOSEPH CHINARD, 1756-1813

MME RÉCAMIER. (1777-1849; Jeanne Françoise Julie Adélaïde.) Formerly in the Penha Longa Collection.

Terracotta. H. 25 3/16 in. Executed about 1805. Signed: *Chinard a lyon* (in front); *Chinard/de l institut/et de l athenée/De lyon* (in back).

Lent by the Musée Cognacq-Jay

OF THIS BOOK
2,000 COPIES WERE PRINTED
NOVEMBER, 1935
PLANTIN PRESS
NEW YORK